THE SNOWSHOE PRIEST

Written by Elizabeth Fust

Illustrated by Olivia Theut

With the Bishop Baraga Association

The Snowshoe Priest

Copyright © 2023 Elizabeth Fust

No part of this work may be reproduced in any form or by any electronic or mechanical means, including information storage and retrieval systems, without written permission in writing from the author, except brief quotations for review purposes.

Editing by Jansina of Rivershore Books
Illustrations by Olivia Theut

Library of Congress Control Number: 2023920781

ISBN: 979-8-21831-125-4

Printed in the United States of America
10   9   8   7   6   5   4   3   2

Rivershore Books
8982 Van Buren St. NE • Minneapolis, MN 55434
612-208-3434 • info@rivershorebooks.com

THE SNOWSHOE PRIEST

Written By
Elizabeth Fust

Illustrated By
Olivia Theut

With
**Len McKeen and the
Bishop Baraga Association**

Unum est necessarium.

"Only one thing is necessary:

to love and serve God, and each other." (Luke 10:42)

Bishop Baraga's motto on his coat of arms

On a hill looking over Lake Superior, not far from St. Peter Cathedral, there used to be the home of a very holy, special man.

His name was Frederic Baraga. But everyone called him the Snowshoe Priest.

Frederic's house is a museum now and when you visit, Joe, the museum guide, greets you.

"Would you like a tour?" he asks.

As you start the tour, Joe says, "Long before Bishop Frederic Baraga lived in this house and before he was a Bishop, as a little boy Frederic lived in a manor house in a land called Slovenia."

Frederic had two sisters: an older sister named Amalia and a younger sister named Antonia.

Their parents taught them about God's love for them and how to be kind and generous to others so they could love others like God does. Because of this, Frederic had a habit of giving his shoes away to other people who didn't have any.

Ever since he was a little boy, Frederic liked to pray and talk to God, the saints, and especially Mother Mary. Frederic also liked playing outside, as well as reading and learning new languages.

His native language was Slovenian and he learned German, French, English, Latin, and Greek for a school examination.

When he was older, he studied to become a priest, then Frederic was called Father Baraga.

As a priest, Father Baraga would wake up very early in the morning so he could pray for three hours before starting work for the day at sunrise.

He would often pray to Mother Mary, asking her to keep him safe and help him be brave while he served her son, Jesus Christ.

Joe tells you that when Father Baraga was a priest in Slovenia, he helped rebuild a church. He built many things, including stations of the cross and even tabernacles. He also wrote many books, including a big book of his favorite prayers, to help others pray and become closer to God.

A Bishop in Cincinnati, Ohio, was asking for priests from around the world to come to America; they needed them to teach the faith across the land.

In 1830, when he was thirty-three years old, Father Baraga left to go to the Great Lakes region. He said goodbye to his family and friends in Slovenia and went on a ship to the new country. It took thirty days for the ship to cross the ocean from Europe to the New World, as they called America.

Father Baraga was sent to the Ojibwe tribe to minister, and they were excited to welcome him to their community. He wanted to learn their language, Ojibwe, so he could speak and pray with the people he met in their own language.

In the museum there is a painting of Father Baraga wearing black, looking very different from his Ojibwe friend "The people Father Baraga met called him a "black robe" because he, and other priests who taught the faith to Native Americans, wore black robes," Joe explains.

Towns weren't close to each other in those days. Father Baraga would have to walk for a very long time to visit his friends.

He walked through swamps, used trees as bridges, and trudged through snow drifts so he could bring Jesus to everyone. It took a very long time to travel, and Father Baraga would say prayers along the whole way.

In the museum, Joe shows you some heavy snowshoes made of wood that are longer than some children are tall!

Joe says, "because they are big and flat they can help people walk on top of the snow. It often snowed so much in Michigan that the snow would pile up taller than a person!"

Father Baraga and the guides who traveled with him needed these snowshoes to reach people as they shared God's love, so people called him the Snowshoe Priest.

One day, Fr. Baraga had been walking from one town to another when the weather became so awful that he got lost. In the middle of the snow storm he sat down on a log to pray knowing God would help him find the way.

14

A fellow named Mr. LeMoine found Fr. Baraga, who was very cold and had been outside for a very long time. Mr. LeMoine led Fr. Baraga out of the storm and took him home. As a thank you for taking care of him, Fr. Baraga gave Mr. LeMoine the crucifix he was wearing.

"People still pray with that crucifix," Joe says, "when they need God's help and to find His way."

The Native Americans helped Father Baraga build churches all over Michigan. They built them out of the pine trees that grow there.

"Sometimes they also built one-room schoolhouses, homes, and gardens," Joe says.

"Father Baraga would teach the children before sending them home to share what they learned with their families. He taught them many things, including how to read and write Ojibwe, and then how to read and write English. Like his parents taught him, Father Baraga shared with the children about God's love for us. He taught them to be kind and generous to others. Most importantly he taught them to love others like God does."

There are lots of lakes and rivers in the Great Lakes region. Father Baraga borrowed a birch bark canoe so he could travel faster to meet more people by traveling on the rivers and lakes to see them.

He took a guide with him to help along the way. Sometimes the water was dangerous and they would pray to God and Mother Mary to keep them safe. They always thanked God for keeping them safe on their travels.

The new friends he met in America called Father Baraga the messenger of the Great Spirit. Joe tells you that the Great Spirit is what the Native Americans called the Master of Life.

Father Baraga was often busy traveling to visit people, but when he wasn't traveling, he wrote more books. He wrote a dictionary of the Ojibwe language that he was learning from his new friends.

In the museum, Joe shows you a special vestment called a chasuble that is covered in colorful flower patterns. He tells you that to say thank you to Father Baraga, his Native American friends made him this chasuble to wear to Mass. It is made out of deerskin and dyed using berries and plants, and even copper, which are all found in Michigan.

Their gift was very important because they could have used the deerskin for items they needed for their families, but they chose to make something beautiful for their special friend in gratitude for all he had done and to honor and thank God for sending them their holy friend.

Word spread of Father Baraga's good work teaching the faith. So many priests and seminarians were following in his footsteps and coming to the Great Lakes region that they needed someone's guidance for the work to continue.

24

Because of this, the Pope made Father Baraga a Bishop in charge of the priests and seminarians, which meant he could help even more people.

25

So many people were coming to church that they didn't all fit in the building anymore. They needed to build an even bigger church, but they didn't have the supplies. Bishop Baraga knew where he could go for help. He was going to raise money to expand the mission as more and more people kept coming to the faith.

Bishop Baraga traveled across the ocean back to Slovenia.
He had family and friends there who could give him the
money he needed to buy supplies to build a church
because they also
wanted to help
share God's
love.

While he was in Europe, Bishop Baraga was invited to celebrate the wedding of an Emperor and Empress. They gave him a golden chalice to use in his churches. He had been given treasures by many people and sold them to buy supplies for his communities, but he kept the chalice. "And it is still being used in the Diocese of Marquette today, more than 175 years later!" Joe tells you.

It was hard to be away from his children, which is what Bishop Baraga called the people to whom he taught the faith. When it was finally time for Bishop Baraga to come back to Michigan, he brought his younger sister Antonia with him. She also wanted to help the people in America learn about God's love.

Bishop Baraga loved learning and sharing the faith since he was a little boy. He wanted everyone to know God's love, and the love of Mother Mary and the saints. When he grew up he got to travel to America and help the people there. Bishop Baraga lived a long time ago, and his good works go on still.

"Have you heard his name before?" Joe asks. "Many schools, roads, and parks are named after him to honor him. His legacy lives on in the churches he built and the Diocese of Marquette that he helped establish."

As you stand out in the garden by the house, Joe tells you one more thing.

"Bishop Baraga's mission in life was to know and serve the Lord with all his heart, all his soul, and all his mind and to bring others to the faith so they might come to know and serve the Lord who loves us.

Bishop Baraga knew that all we need is God, which is why his motto is 'Only one thing is necessary.'

He taught us that when we know that, our job is to pray for others to help them get to heaven. Now that you know his story, keep our good friend Bishop Baraga in your prayers."

PRAYER FOR BISHOP BARAGA'S CAUSE FOR CANONIZATION

O God, thank you for the life and holiness of your servant, Frederic Baraga.

I pray you will honor him by the title of Saint. He dedicated himself completely to missionary activity to make you known, loved, and served by the people who you love. As a man of peace and love, Baraga brought peace and love wherever he traveled.

Lord, grant Venerable Bishop Baraga the grace of beatification.

We ask this in Christ's name.

Amen

CAUSE FOR CANONIZATION

The Bishop Baraga Association was established in 1930 to promote the Cause for Beatification and Canonization of Bishop Frederic Baraga. In 1952, the Bishop of Marquette appointed a historical commission to collect and catalog material pertinent for the Cause of Beatification for Bishop Baraga. In 2012, Pope Benedict XVI declared Bishop Frederic Baraga "Venerable."

As Joe said in the book, many have prayed for Venenerable Bishop Baraga's intercession will praying with the crucifix Bishop Baraga gave Mr. LeMoine. Many of these prayers with the crucifix support his cause for canonization.

You can prayerfully support Bishop Baraga's Cause for Canonization by praying the prayer for canonization daily, asking for Bishop Baraga's intercession for your prayers. You can also regularly pray the Baraga Novena, which can be found at bishopbaraga.org or by contacting the Bishop Baraga Association. You can further show your support of Bishop Baraga by becoming a member of the Bishop Baraga Association at bishopbaraga.org.

BiSHOP BARAGA YOUTH PROGRAM

Children can become members of the Bishop Baraga Association as well. Their membership continues until their 18th birthday. They will receive regular youth bulletins full of educational information about Venerable Bishop Baraga along with fun activities.

Bishop Baraga Association
Baraga Educational Center and Museum
615 S. Fourth Street
Marquette, MI 49855
BishopBaragaAssoc@gmail.com
www.bishopbaraga.org
906-227-9117

ACKNOWLEDGMENTS

Special thanks go to Lenora McKeen, Executive Director of the Bishop Baraga Association, as well as the Bishop Baraga Association Advisory Board.

Thank you to everyone who read drafts of this book and provided feedback: the Murphy family, the Scibelli family, Carley Challender, Doc Surrell, Jamie Gualdoni, Hattie Hanold, and Abby Trefilek.

Thank you to Jansina Grossman at Rivershore Books for editing and creating the layout of this book.

ABOUT THE AUTHOR AND ILLUSTRATOR

Elizabeth Fust, like Bishop Baraga, is not from the U.P. but chose to make it her home. She now lives in Marquette not far from Lake Superior and the Bishop Baraga House. She is the author of *The Hungry Kitten's Tale* and *Wooly and the Good Shepherd* Bible story picture books.

Olivia Theut grew up in the Upper Peninsula. She now resides in Gladstone where she is a Clinical Social Worker. Olivia enjoys making art in her free time. *The Snowshoe Priest* is the first book she has illustrated.

Can you find the 7 hidden clan animals? Look for the Crane, Bear, Marten, Eagle, Deer, Loon, and Turtle! The different clans represent the different traditional roles and responsibilities in society.

RIVERSHORE BOOKS

www.rivershorebooks.com

info@rivershorebooks.com